MAKING A BETTER WORLD

Natural Foods and Products

By Gary Chandler and Kevin Graham

Twenty-First Century Books
A Division of Henry Holt and Company
New York

Twenty-First Century Books
A division of Henry Holt and Company, Inc.
115 West 18th Street
New York, New York 10011

Henry Holt® and colophon are registered trademarks of
Henry Holt and Company, Inc.
Publishers since 1866

Published in Canada by Fitzhenry & Whiteside Ltd.
195 Allstate Parkway, Markham, Ontario L3R 4T8

Printed in the United States of America on acid free paper.

Created and produced in association with Blackbirch Graphics, Inc.
Series Editor: Tanya Lee Stone

Library of Congress Cataloging-in-Publication Data

Chandler, Gary.
   Natural foods and products / by Gary Chandler and Kevin Graham. —
1st ed.
         p.   cm. — (Making a better world)
   Includes bibliographical references and index.
   Summary: Relates success stories about people who apply innovative
techniques to produce natural foods and products that protect the environment and save money and energy.
   ISBN 0-8050-4623-2
   1. Organic farming—Juvenile literature. 2. Organic gardening—Juvenile literature. 3. Natural foods—Juvenile literature. 4. Green products—
Juvenile literature. [1. Organic farming. 2. Organic gardening. 3. Natural
foods. 4. Gardening.] I. Graham, Kevin. II. Title. III. Series: Making a
better world (New York, N.Y.)
S605.5.C42   1996
333.76'16—dc20   96-15565
                                                                    CIP
                                                                    AC

Table of Contents

Welcome to
Making a Better World

We know that humans' food supply depends on a healthy environment—yet we continue to allow food production to take a toll on our natural resources. Literally tons of insecticides are applied to crops around the world every year. These toxins, or poisons, frequently end up in the water we drink and the food we eat. Forests have been, and continue to be, leveled for agriculture and other purposes. The soil erosion that results from this deforestation adds up. Eventually, valuable topsoil is carried into the oceans, where it alters those ecosystems. Elsewhere, more forests are leveled to create the packaging for our food supply. And finally, the food industries consume massive amounts of energy transporting tons of food to every grocery store.

Of course, everyone—billions of people—around the world must eat every day. The industries that meet this demand can make a big difference in the environment—in either positive or negative ways. They can help by minimizing their negative impact on the natural world.

Much of the responsibility for positive change rests with those involved in these industries. But a great challenge also falls to consumers—people like you who buy products. If we insist that the products and services we buy be produced in an environmentally responsible way, companies will eventually find ways to do this.

All of the books in *Making a Better World* report on people—kids, parents, schools, neighborhoods, and companies—who have decided to get involved in a cause they believe in. Through their dedication, commitment, and dreams, they helped to make ours a better world. Each one of the stories in this book will take you through the steps of what it took for some ordinary people to achieve something extraordinary. Of course, in the space of one book, we can share only a fraction of the wonderful stories that exist. After a long and complicated selection process, we have chosen what we believe are the most exciting subjects to tell you about.

We hope this book will encourage you to learn more about natural foods and products. Better yet, we hope all the books in this series inspire you to get involved. There are plenty of ways that each individual—including you—can make a better world. You will find some opportunities throughout this book—and there are many others out there waiting for you to discover. If you would like to write to us for more information, the address is Earth News, P.O. Box 101413, Denver, CO 80250.

Sincerely,

Gary Chandler
and
Kevin Graham

Organic Agriculture

Crop production is an essential part of life. The way it is done can have a big impact on the environment. Water use, pesticides, chemical fertilizers, groundwater pollution, erosion, rainforest destruction, poverty, and starvation are just a few of the issues related to this topic. It's a complicated topic, because food is essential to life. With more and more lives on Earth to sustain, efficient food production per acre is becoming increasingly important every day. However, organic farming and biological pest control offer ways to minimize the negative impact of agriculture and lawn and garden maintenance. Organic farmers don't use chemical fertilizers or pesticides. Since these toxic chemicals often leave residue on fruits and vegetables, and can also cause water pollution, many farmers have found a market for foods grown without them. Biological pest control also relies on natural insect repellents instead of toxic chemicals. These practices can save farmers money and keep toxins out of the food chain—the order in which organisms feed on one another in an ecosystem. The success stories in this chapter present just a few of the organic alternatives available to us.

Mother Nature Colors Cotton

In Arizona, one enterprising business is actually growing cotton in living color! This unique cotton does not need to be dyed. What began as a plant-breeding hobby eventually turned into an environmentally beneficial business for Sally Fox. She developed cotton plants that grow colored cotton right on the stalk. Now she sells this special product to companies such as Esprit, L.L. Bean, and Levi's, sparing the companies the need to bleach and dye the cotton before manufacturing clothing.

Initially, Fox worked in entomology, the study of insects. By researching them, she hoped to find ways to reduce the use of pesticides—poisons meant to kill insect pests—in farming. While breeding cotton plants for pest resistance in 1982, she came across some cotton seeds covered with a beautiful brown lint (visible fibers on the seeds' exteriors). Excitedly, Fox asked the cotton breeder she worked for if she could research the possibility of growing colored cotton. He responded that no one wanted brown cotton and that she would have to do the research on her own time.

Fox took the challenge. She searched for seeds that had nicely colored lint and planted them in pots. While the plants produced colored cotton as she had hoped, the material's fibers were too short for use in the spinning machines required for the manufacture of cloth.

Fox embarked on a cross-pollination breeding program. She bred the colored plants with white cotton plants that had longer, higher-quality fibers. By 1988, she had developed machine-spinnable, colored cotton that met many industry standards.

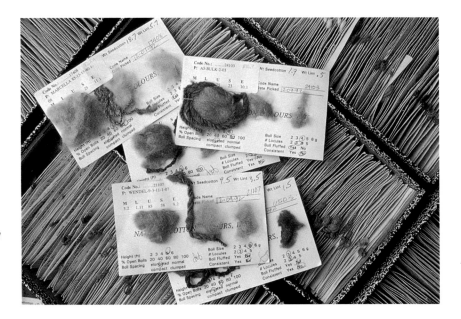

Fibers are carefully tested and sorted to find the best cotton from each crop.

Today, Fox's breeding efforts continue on 50 acres of land near Wickenburg, Arizona, as she works to develop more and more colorful cotton plants. The process requires close attention to detail and is very time-consuming.

Out of 250,000 plants grown in each crop, Fox collects seeds from only the best 3,000 plants to grow the next season. The fibers from these 3,000 plants are tested for length, strength, and other qualities important for spinning. After testing, new seeds from the best 1,000 plants are germinated the following season—and then only 250 seeds from the chosen few will actually be planted.

Fox made a huge breakthrough in 1995, when three new varieties of plants produced high yields of the best-quality fibers to date. These new fibers will allow for faster spinning and overall processing.

For a long time, Fox was not able to fill orders. But she now has a warehouse full of bales of the older versions of her cotton, ready to send to customers. All of her future crops, however, will bloom with the new quality. Fox will take orders from various manufacturers who want the newer cotton for their towels, linens, clothing, and upholstery, and then will contract with farmers in Texas and Arizona to grow the crops. The cotton—sold under the trademark FoxFibre®—is available in varying shades of brown, green, and brownish-red. Interestingly enough, the natural colors in FoxFibre® actually deepen after washings.

Most clothing companies must first bleach white cotton to prepare it for dyes. After dyeing, finishing chemicals are used to secure the colors so that they won't run when applied to cotton. Dyes and chemicals cause companies two problems: They pollute water and cost money. In making yarn, if a textile mill pays a dollar to buy the cotton and another dollar to spin it, it will then have to pay an additional $2 to dye it.

Not only are the dyes themselves expensive, but plenty of energy, water, and the treatment of wastewater is needed to complete the process. In much of the developing world, where wastewater treatment is not performed, the dyes and

Sally Fox inspects one of her beautiful fields of environmentally friendly cotton.

chemicals used in the making of clothing simply add to pollution. But cotton grown naturally with color eliminates the wastes created by these processes and saves the companies both energy and water costs.

"You can now have color without using any dyes," Fox says. "This has made people reconsider the use of chemicals and how they can improve the production process from the farm to the store. We're still at the beginning of a new field, and we're just starting to understand all there is to learn. But it's definitely a step in the right direction."

The only real drawback to Fox's effort is the use of increasingly scarce water to grow crops in the dry climate of Arizona and Texas. In California, where Fox began her venture, she installed water-saving irrigation equipment, cutting her water use in half. But enough money needs to be made in order to purchase similar equipment for her Arizona operation. "The challenge is to do it sensibly and be as careful and environmentally responsible as possible."

To that end, Fox's operation involves strictly organic farming practices. These organic methods are certified in Texas by the state's department of agriculture and in Arizona by the Organic Crop Improvement Association. "If you can farm without them [toxic chemicals and fertilizers], why not?" she points out.

In the future, Fox hopes that her cotton will be seen for what it is—a less-expensive alternative. "We've made a lot of progress, but my goal is that my colors will replace dyes," she says. "And economically, they should. It is simply a cheaper alternative for any product. For certain color ranges, Fox-Fibre® provides a cost-saving option to make products in a way that doesn't add to the chemical burden."

For More Information

Write to Natural Cotton Colours Inc./FoxFibre®, P.O. Box 66, Wickenburg, AZ 85358, or call (520) 684–7199.

Good Insects Fight Off Bad Ones

A Maryland company has developed an alternative to insecticides by sending beneficial insects to battle harmful ones. Nematodes are microscopic worms that can be grown and used as natural insecticides. Certain types of beneficial nematodes were identified more than 60 years ago and have been tested for more than a decade. The biosys Company recently perfected a system of growing the organisms and packaging them in a formula that keeps the nematodes alive for five or six months. The concept for biosys came from the U.S. Department of Agriculture (USDA). Through a licensing agreement with the USDA, biosys markets the technology.

"We've been researching this idea for the last seven or eight years," says David Judd, vice-president of marketing. "And we are now the world leader in the use of nematodes as insecticides."

The company's products can control dozens of unwanted insects that attack grass, shrubs, fruit trees, flower beds, and vegetable gardens. Grubs, cutworms, and root weevils are among the most destructive insect varieties. The nematodes are lethal to these "bad" bugs. But the nematodes won't harm humans, animals, groundwater, or even other beneficial insects such as earthworms, ladybugs, and honey bees.

The nematodes are part of the natural predator/prey relationship in the soil ecosystem, where many insects spend much of their lives. The nematodes track their prey through various means, including insects' carbon dioxide and waste emissions.

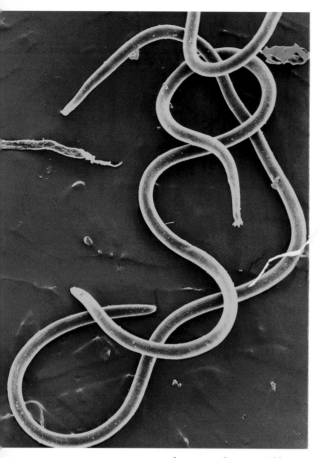

Nematodes, shown here with false-color imaging, are used as natural insecticides.

Nematodes enter an insect's body through natural openings and release deadly bacteria inside the insect. The organisms then reproduce inside the host body, creating a new generation of beneficial nematodes. Once the insects have been fatally poisoned, the nematodes die.

Unlike many chemical insecticides, which are usually effective for just a few days, a nematode application can last five or six weeks. The majority of the wormlike creatures are microscopic, not visible to the naked eye.

The U.S. Environmental Protection Agency (EPA) has exempted nematodes from normal registration requirements because they are harmless and are naturally occurring organisms. Because the nematode products are not chemicals, treated land can be used immediately after spraying.

"Our products eliminate or cut down substantially on the use of chemical insecticides," Judd says. "This means far fewer problems with chemical residue affecting produce, farm workers, or communities in agricultural areas. A number of large chemical companies are now interested in this type of insect control. They realize this is the new wave of insecticides and can see that in ten years, many of their current products will be outdated."

For More Information

Write to biosys Company, 10150 Old Columbia Road, Columbia, MD 21046, or call (410) 381-2800.

Solid Wastes Serve as Fertilizer

Treated wastewater solids from New York, Baltimore, Los Angeles, and other cities throughout the United States are making farmers more productive. By taking part in a unique recycling and agriculture program, the farmers are receiving nutrient-rich biosolids and are having the material spread over their land as an organic fertilizer—all free of charge. The biosolids—which are treated to reduce volume, destroy harmful bacteria, and reduce odor—not only fertilize the soil with nutrients but can also boost its water-holding capacity, increase plant growth, and reduce erosion.

The Bio Gro Division of Wheelabrator Water Technologies in Annapolis, Maryland, now has several hundred contracts with various cities to manage their biosolids—the solids produced by wastewater treatment. The company has permits to disperse the more than 1 million acres of agricultural land as fertilizer. "We're paid by the cities—the generators of the solids—to recycle the material," says Jane Forste, Bio Gro's vice-president of Technical Services. "We provide processing transportation, permitting, monitoring, and application of the material for the farmers." As landfills across the nation continue to fill up, beneficial uses for biosolids produced by wastewater treatment plants are welcome. And by helping to fertilize farmland, the company is also reducing the amount of chemical fertilizers that farmers use to replenish their soil.

To conduct these programs with farmers, Bio Gro must operate under regulations set up by the U.S. Environmental

Left: An unproductive field before the application of biosolids. *Right:* The same field after benefiting from the organic waste.

Protection Agency (EPA) as well as by various state and local agencies. These regulations ensure that agricultural, environmental, and health considerations are addressed. The EPA requires that trace metals and other by-products of industry be removed from wastewater before it is sent to treatment plants. Bio Gro also provides independent operating, testing, and monitoring of all aspects of the entire treatment process to ensure safe land application.

Trucks deliver the biosolids as a liquid or semi-solid material to the farms, where it is applied to the surface of the land through spraying or spreading. It can also be mixed with the soil by injection or plowing. Bio Gro's staff coordinates all phases of the operations, working closely with farmers to apply the biosolids in accordance with crop schedules and fertilization requirements. Also, because the application of biosolids promotes rapid growth of grasses and other vegetation, it has been used successfully in land reclamation projects to revitalize areas damaged by strip mining. Bio Gro is now helping thousands of farmers in more than 20 states save money on fertilizer and improve their crop yields through its land-application business.

For More Information

Write to Wheelabrator Water Technologies, Bio Gro Division, 180 Admiral Cochrane Drive, Suite 305, Annapolis, MD 21401, or call (410) 224–0022.

Serving a Just Cup
of Java

Coffee (sometimes referred to as java) is the world's most heavily traded food commodity and the primary export crop of more than 60 nations. As such, it is steeped in environmental and human-rights issues across the globe—particularly in the developing world, where nearly all coffee crops are grown.

Because it takes the average annual yield of one tree to make just one pound of coffee, the huge task of producing and harvesting a crop for coffee drinkers around the world requires the toil of millions of farm workers. Most of these workers are very poor. Most have no access to clean water, proper health care, adequate education, or decent homes. What is more, the workers and their families must often live in a contaminated and depleted environment.

A majority of coffee farming today, like so many other forms of agriculture, relies heavily on the use of chemical fertilizers and pesticides. On small farms, the farmers apply these dangerous chemicals themselves. On large plantations, farm workers typically are responsible for applying the chemicals. They often do so without the benefit of equipment to safeguard their health or even with the knowledge that the chemicals are dangerous. The cost to human life and to the ecosystem is significant. This is especially true in countries where chemical use is not regulated and where older products that are barred from use in the United States are still used.

Several efforts are now under way to improve these distressing conditions in the coffee-producing world.

Coffee is sorted and separated at a cooperative in Guatemala.

For example, co-founders Joan and Paul Katzeff of the Thanksgiving Coffee Company don't want you to just have a cup of coffee; they want you to enjoy a "just cup"—as in justice for coffee farmers and the environment. Through the company's coffee sales, it supports organic coffee growers in various parts of the developing world. And by working with collectives and cooperatives (families who grow crops together) to ensure that the coffee is grown without chemical pesticides or fertilizers, the Thanksgiving Coffee Company helps farmers use energy-efficient and sustainable-agriculture methods.

Says Paul Katzeff, "More than 40 million gallons of pesticides are used each year on coffee crops around the world, not to mention all the chemical fertilizers that are used. Certified organic coffee is a way for me to take my ecological and social concerns, weave them into one package, and create a socially and environmentally sound approach to gourmet coffee."

The company pays 40 to 75 percent above the market value for its organic coffee beans. Organically grown coffee requires much more labor-intensive farming for tasks such as composting, pruning, and weeding. By supporting small cooperatives— where much of the world's more ecologically minded coffee is produced—the company is also helping small farms to band together and compete in the marketplace. By working together in cooperatives, these small farms can combine their resources to handle their processing and transportation needs.

Katzeff has created a set of standards for coffee purchasing, which is part of the company's buying effort. This involves granting a "seal of approval" placed on packages that are filled with equitably traded, organically grown coffee. Thirteen criteria are applied for its so-called sustainable coffee—that is, coffee that is produced in environmentally sound ways. If a farm scores at least ten points from the criteria, the coffee is eligible for purchase by Thanksgiving. The single largest point-scoring measure, which receives five points, involves growing coffee the traditional way—in the shade under the rainforest canopy. Organically grown and certified coffee scores three points; while sun-dried, small-farm–grown, or cooperative-member–produced coffee adds one point each.

By promoting this seal of approval, Katzeff hopes to prompt more U.S. coffee importers to operate in a socially responsible manner and help consumers understand the workings of the coffee industry in the developing world. "Since most coffee is exported to industrialized countries of the North, retailers and consumers play a large role in how coffee is marketed, and, therefore, how coffee is produced," Katzeff says. "By

Paul Katzeff teaches coffee roasting techniques to members of cooperatives.

Paul Katzeff enjoys a "just cup" of java.

enabling consumers to choose sustainable coffee through their daily purchases, we can advance the consumption and production of fairly traded and environmentally friendly coffee."

Thanksgiving Coffee's oldest and most aggressive program to promote "a just cup" involves the creation of consumer rebates to growers of sustainable coffees. Begun in 1985, Thanksgiving Coffee Company puts aside 15 cents for each pound of organically grown coffee sold. In Mexico, these funds are then administered by another organization, called Coffee Kids, for which Katzeff was an adviser from 1989 to 1995. Coffee Kids spends these funds from Thanksgiving Coffee on programs that help improve the living conditions for children and families in coffee-producing communities. In Peru, rebate funds totalling $17,000 were used by the Organic Farmers Cooperative to purchase land and to build an award-winning laboratory that breeds a fungus to control a pest, the coffee tree borer, biologically instead of with pesticides. In Nicaragua, Thanksgiving Coffee Company has supported the National Farm Workers Union coffee farms with rebates that come from the company's "Coffee for Peace" packages of Nicaraguan coffee.

For More Information

Write to the Thanksgiving Coffee Company, P.O. Box 1918, Fort Bragg, CA 95437, or call (800) 648–6491. You can also send e-mail at tcc.mcn.org

Coffee Kids

A nonprofit group called Coffee Kids, formed in 1989, is also helping change the coffee industry. Coffee Kids wants families and communities in the coffee-growing world to be given the chance to improve both their lives and their environment. Out of economic necessity, many children in coffee-producing nations are put to work as soon as farmers are willing to pay them or as soon as they can help on the family farm. Children typically begin working by age ten, sacrificing their education around the fourth or fifth grade.

In 1984, Coffee Kids' founder, Bill Fishbein, had started a small coffee shop in Providence, Rhode Island. He finally started making a decent income from the business in the late 1980s. Then he read several John Steinbeck novels, finishing with *The Grapes of Wrath*. "That book carved something into my heart. I saw a connection between the characters in the novel and the migrant coffee workers who were responsible for my financial independence," he explains. "I decided to do something."

During a trip to Guatemala, Fishbein witnessed the situation firsthand. What he discovered there changed his life. Living and environmental conditions in the coffee-growing areas that he visited were worse than he anticipated. And he was shocked at how difficult it was for families to make a decent living, and the toll this took on the environment.

When he returned from Guatemala, Fishbein started Coffee Kids. Initially, Coffee Kids worked to get businesses and individuals to sponsor children whose families depended on coffee crops for a living—the "coffee kids." "I saw it as a way to give something back to these communities. Children in coffee communities could easily be identified and sponsored," Fishbein says.

Coffee Kids' activities have also broadened. Money is collected from businesses and consumers through membership dues, general contributions, coin-drop donations, and the sale of promotional material such as T-shirts and coffee mugs. These funds are applied to numerous projects in nine coffee-growing countries. The projects address concerns such as sanitation, health care, nutrition, education, entrepreneurial efforts, and the environment. "Our work is to bridge the economic gap between coffee consumers and producers," Fishbein comments.

A new type of coffee dryer, which will give small farms more freedom in the marketplace, is also being supported by Coffee Kids. Coffee-drying techniques have changed little over the past century, but this small, solar-powered dryer will

Bill Fishbein visits with a family in a Guatemalan coffee-producing community.

allow small farms to dry their freshly picked berries within the 24- to 36-hour time frame required before the berries spoil. Once in their dried form, the berries can be stored until the farmer chooses to sell them. The new dryer is being tested in Guatemala and its neighbor Honduras. If it proves efficient and reliable, farmers will be able to lease or purchase the dryers for their farms.

In addition, Coffee Kids works with local farmers to help them better understand the detrimental effects of erosion and chemicals, as well as the benefits of naturally increasing the health of the soil. Alley cropping, for instance, is a method of farming in which different crops are planted in the rows between coffee trees. Planting peas or beans in the rows helps to nourish the soil, which in turn nourishes the coffee trees. The farmers benefit, too, from a broader diet.

Finally, Coffee Kids promotes other forms of crop diversification along with its organic coffee-farming efforts. In fact, today, the communities that the organization works with in Mexico grow only organic coffee. "There's now a tremendous sense on the part of the farmers that their lives are being harmed. These people have always thought that the only way to produce enough coffee was to use a lot of chemicals, but they're rethinking this practice," Fishbein says.

"Helping communities in all these various efforts is a complicated and delicate business, and must be done with respect so that dignity is not lost, dependency not created, and cultural aspects not disturbed," Fishbein explains. "We want to promote the process of sound and respectful development, but we must go slowly and at the community's pace. We're in it for the long run and have the patience to sow the seeds and gradually let them germinate."

For More Information

Write to Coffee Kids, 207 Wickenden Street, Providence, RI 02903, or call (800) 334–9099.

Growing Grapes Organically

Fetzer Vineyards, the nation's sixth-largest producer of premium wines, is going organic. The California company is the first major U.S. winery to sell wines with labels that state "Produced from organically farmed Mendocino County grapes." Sold under the name Bonterra, which loosely means "good earth," one is a white wine, the other a red wine. Both have received good reviews, and the company plans to expand its list of organic labels.

The company started organically growing grapes in the mid-1980s. By combining French intensive-gardening practices with other organic efforts, Fetzer eventually created a unique way to grow grapes naturally. To control insects, predatory wasps replaced pesticides, and composted grape seeds and skins helped eliminate the need for fertilizers. Another key component of the effort involved new weeding machines, which weed the rows between the vines as well as around the vines themselves. They gently "feel" around the vines by using devices similar to the "curb-feelers" found on some cars.

"Developing these machines took time, energy, and money, but after three years, our costs dropped drastically," explains Fetzer Vineyard's Public Relations Director George Rose. "Now, farming without chemicals actually costs less." By not using pesticides and herbicides on the grapevines, Fetzer was able to eliminate its insurance costs related to spraying the chemicals and provide safer working conditions and cleaner surrounding water resources.

A Fetzer employee smiles as a new crop of organic grapes is harvested.

Currently, Fetzer farms 360 acres of organic grapes, certified by California Certified Organic Farmers (CCOF), a third-party inspection organization. (Before land can be certified by CCOF, it must be farmed under organic regulations for three years.) Another 1,100 acres are farmed by the Fetzer family.

"Our goal is to grow or buy 100 percent organically grown grapes by the year 2000," says Paul Dolan, Fetzer's president. "This is not an idealistic goal, but one based on a consumer demand for a healthier product."

Fetzer Vineyards has taken other important measures to help the environment. During the past three years, it has cut its landfill dumping fees by 80 percent through a composting effort. Each year, Fetzer composts about 20,000 tons of grape skins, seeds, and stems, along with various other materials. The nutrient-rich mixture is then used as fertilizer in the company's organic farming effort.

For More Information

On Fetzer's organic efforts, write to Fetzer Vineyards, P.O. Box 611, Hopland, CA 95449. For general information about the company, call (800) 846–8637.

Natural Gardens
Improve Communities

We have learned that large farms—and agriculture in general—can protect the environment by using fewer chemical fertilizers and pesticides and by applying some innovative techniques. But communities can also make a big impact on the environment. People can work together to improve the overall quality of life in an area, for example, by involving community members in a "grassroots" effort to provide food, jobs, and a prettier neighborhood. You and your family can also save money on food and can eat healthier produce by keeping a small organic garden. Keeping pesticides and chemical fertilizers out of your yard also makes it a safer place for your family and pets to live.

Giving Homeless Hands Green Thumbs

Increasing the amount of green space in the concrete jungles of urban society is a difficult task, but with the help of several homeless people, Sandy Beldon is bringing new life to New York City.

In 1991, Beldon, a senior vice-president of Rodale Press, began volunteering at a homeless shelter. One day, Beldon crawled through a broken window and on to the shelter's roof. He looked at the piles of trash and broken glass sparkling in the sunlight on the roof and saw a garden waiting to happen— as well as a chance to help the homeless people at the shelter.

"I thought this would be a great place for a large vegetable garden—providing food for the kitchen, engaging the interest of the homeless people, and teaching a few people the basics of organic gardening," Beldon explains. "And it could provide the homeless center with revenue from the sale of produce grown on the roof." In addition, the large garden would help the atmosphere through the process of absorbing carbon dioxide and emitting oxygen.

Beldon convinced the St. Agnes Center, which owned the building, to give the garden a try. Rodale Press, a major publisher of health- and fitness-oriented books and magazines, including *Organic Gardening*, donated the necessary materials.

To start the rooftop garden, nine tons of seeds, plants, compost, mulch, and specially mixed garden soil were transported up seven flights of stairs. By June 1992, more than 100 wooden tubs, each four feet wide by four feet long, were on

Above: *The roof of this New York City homeless shelter was transformed into a highly productive organic garden.* ***Below:*** *The food from the garden is eaten at the shelter and is sold at a nearby produce cart.*

the tennis-court–size roof, ready for planting. Vegetables such as broccoli, carrots, and tomatoes were planted, along with herbs including such favorites as basil, oregano, and rosemary.

"Our goal in planting and gardening is to empower the homeless to do more for themselves," Beldon says. "By providing the materials and teaching them gardening techniques, they acquire marketable skills."

The garden is part of the Pathway to Employment Program at the Grand Central Partnership, a neighborhood coalition working to improve a 53-block area around New York City's Grand Central Station. To date, eight homeless people who have participated in the Pathway to Employment program have converted their new skills into horticultural and landscaping jobs. Their fellow residents at the shelter are benefiting nutritionally from the fresh, organically grown food. And, as Beldon envisioned, the shelter now sells some of the produce from a cart at nearby Bryant Park, raising money to help support the program.

If the gardening program were replicated across the United States, the cumulative environmental effect could be quite significant. Beldon exclaims, "If we can succeed here in midtown Manhattan, seven stories up in a building without an elevator, we can create gardens in homeless centers and other places across the country."

To keep the momentum rolling, Beldon and Rodale Press started ground-level gardens in Jersey City, New Jersey, and Allentown, Pennsylvania. The effort even resurrected a littered plot of land in Washington, D.C.—at a busy intersection across the street from the Georgetown University Law School—and turned it into an urban garden.

For More Information

About starting a rooftop garden, write to Rodale Press at 33 East Minor Street, Emmaus, PA 18098–0099.

Soil Therapy Yields Larger Crops

Gardening is one of the most popular hobbies in the world. Through their own resourcefulness, gardeners can save money while helping the environment. Now, an intensive gardening method called Biointensive developed by Ecology Action, a nonprofit agriculture group, can help gardeners increase vegetable yields by two to four times as compared to modern farming techniques. The simple agriculture system developed by the founder of Ecology Action's mini-farming program, John Jeavons, can turn a small plot of land into a significant food-producing unit. The system uses a fraction of the water, fertilizer, and energy needed for most other farming practices.

Ecology Action was formed in 1972 as a response to the world hunger problem and the need to find a way for people to feed themselves. The group developed and tested a small-scale food-raising system based on Chinese agricultural techniques used 4,000 years ago. The goal was to give people an alternative for sustainable agriculture in the future, in case the Earth's environmental problems compound and eventually grow into a crisis. "I think the best solution to raising enough food is for more people to raise their food locally on a small-scale basis," Jeavons says.

"Sustainable agriculture involves much more than reducing chemical applications," he explains. "The goal of Biointensive farming is to recycle all nutrients, grow compost crops to build and maintain healthy soil, provide nutritious food for people, and integrate fiber crops and trees into the farm. Sustainable agriculture is a very essential part of building sustainable communities."

Jeavons started a demonstration-and-education garden to test applications of the technique, which is affordable and practical. It is also sustainable, since it relies only on available resources. Jeavons calls the system the Biointensive method—caring for the soil to grow large volumes of food efficiently in small areas. The basics of the Biointensive method are easy to learn and rely on local organic materials to enrich and improve the soil.

Aurelio Mendoza Vazquez learned the Biointensive method and teaches it to his classmates in Chiapas, Mexico.

With the use of large amounts of compost (decomposed food and yard waste) and organic fertilizers such as worm excrement, the soil gains the capacity to grow tremendous amounts of food. According to Ecology Action, with the Biointensive method, an entire year's supply of vegetables and fruits could be grown in a six-month growing season on as little as a 100-square-foot piece of ground.

Jeavons has written a number of books and other materials about the Biointensive method for Ecology Action. The book, *How to Grow More Vegetables*, describes the basic techniques of the system. It is currently used by various organizations, including the Peace Corps and UNICEF, as a training manual for overseas nutrition work. The Biointensive method is now used in 109 countries around the world. In Mexico, thousands of people are using the method to grow food for their families, thanks to the distribution of Ecology Action publications in Spanish. India started a national program in 1990, Kenya has trained more than 55,000 small-scale farmers in the method, and the Philippines has mandated that a national Biointensive education program be taught to all students.

Ecology Action trained intern Joshua Machinga, of Kenya, at the Research Garden in California.

Despite its world-wide impact, Ecology Action has remained small. The heart of the organization is still the group's Research Garden Mini-Farm, nestled in the hills above Willits, in northern California. Although the Research Garden serves primarily as a laboratory, the site is also used to train teachers and practitioners in the Biointensive method.

Mini-farms and gardens can thrive in and near population centers, minimizing the need to transport food over long distances. The energy saved is significant. Depending on the crop grown, Biointensive mini-farms have reported incomes of $5,000 to $200,000 per year on plots no larger than one-quarter acre of planted land. These incomes are earned without the use of fossil fuels, expensive machinery, and high investment costs that are typically associated with commercial agriculture.

For More Information

Write to Ecology Action, 5798 Ridgewood Road, Willits, CA 95490–9730, or call (707) 459–0150.

Vacant Lots Make
Good Gardens

Resourceful gardening has been successfully demonstrated by the city of Newark, New Jersey, where the city and its residents are turning vacant lots into prosperous, blooming gardens. By coupling its urban-gardening program with a leaf-composting project, the city has reduced landfill costs while beautifying plots of land that were once littered eyesores.

"We had an ongoing problem with maintaining these vacant lots because of illegal dumping," said Frank Sudol, who was chief of research and program development for the city's department of engineering. "Through the program, we've stopped the dumping, cut maintenance costs, and put the lots to productive use."

Nearly 1,000 once-vacant lots are now being used by residents and students who adopt the lots, then plant gardens and maintain them as community or school projects. Acquiring rich organic matter through composting—in this case from leaves—is essential to the success of these community gardens, because New Jersey's rocky soil makes growing gardens difficult. Each fall, the city urges Newark residents to perform backyard composting—it even provides free backyard composting units to urban gardeners. Furthermore, the city asks residents who do not garden to rake their leaves to the curb, to be collected there and composted under the program.

Leaves are transported to Newark's composting site, where they are screened, watered, and composted (allowed to decay) in long rows. Eventually, the finished product is hauled back into the urban area, where it helps gardens bloom. "Rather than just hauling all that material to the landfill, we use it internally to enrich the soil and improve the value of our neighborhoods," Sudol said. As an added benefit, more and more residents are now composting on their own and hauling the material to their community gardens.

Students, parents, and schools have transformed many abandoned lots into living laboratories where students learn through active, hands-on experience. The Greater Newark Conservancy (GNC), an organization that promotes environmental education, provides committed schools with the necessary materials and tools to convert the lots into living learning centers. The GNC also trains the teachers to accomplish the objectives of a daily curriculum. As teachers and students learn to grow vegetables, test soil, and compost, they learn about the interdependence within the ecosystem and relate local environmental issues to their experience outdoors. Programs are available for students from grades K-12.

An annual dinner is held each year as part of the program to honor the efforts of Newark's community gardeners. Just

This abandoned Newark city lot was revitalized by the GNC.

Start an Indoor Garden

An egg carton makes a great planter. Pull the lid off the top and keep the bottom half, with the egg "cups." Fill each slot of the egg container with soil from your backyard or potting soil from the store or nursery. Pitch in with two or three friends to each buy one packet of different seeds at the store. Then split the seeds up so that you all have a few of each different kind.

Flowers or plants that grow above ground are best for egg-carton gardens. Ask your parents or teacher for advice and read the labels for plants that will do best in your local and personal growing conditions.

Plant the seeds according to the directions on your seed packet and mark which seeds are in each spot. Place it in or near a window that gets good sunlight. Keep watering it every day or two—or as needed.

Now watch the different species grow and take notes about each one's progress. Each type will grow at a different pace and take on different appearances. After the plants begin to outgrow the egg carton, transplant them either outside or to a larger in-door pot. Plants are good for your home because they purify the air—they absorb carbon dioxide and emit oxygen.

before the dinner, people are taken on a bus tour to visit the now-prosperous lots, and a panel of judges chooses winners in various categories. "We're talking about a significant amount of acreage being gardened that would otherwise sit unused," Sudol said. "The program has helped raise community spirit and involvement. About $750,000 worth of produce is grown on Newark's vacant lots each year."

For More Information
Write to the City of Newark, City Hall, 920 Broad Street, Room 410, Newark, NJ 07102, or call (201) 733–8520.

Zoo Animals Generate Valuable Fertilizer

Leaves and other yard wastes are not the only form of natural waste that can be composted. Zoos around the United States are joining in an effort to compost the tons of manure created by their animals.

While visiting Singapore in 1990, Pierce Ledbetter saw elephant dung being sold as compost at numerous garden shops and nurseries. He noticed that it fetched twice the price of other types of compost. Elephant manure, it turns out, has a high level of nitrogen due to the animals' diet, and is therefore more beneficial as compost. Having been involved with the Composting Research Center at New York's Cornell University, Ledbetter soon developed a composting idea called Zoo Doo.

He approached the Memphis (Tennessee) Zoo about the possibility of composting the zoo animals' manure and selling it. Zoo officials immediately raised a number of objections—composting would require too much time and effort, the process would be too smelly, and no one would want the end result. "So I said, 'Let me address these issues,' and in the end, they agreed to give it a shot," Ledbetter explains. "I agreed to take care of both the composting and marketing."

It took six months of composting to produce the first batch of benign-smelling Zoo Doo. When a Memphis newspaper did a story to announce the effort, the first batch sold out in the first weekend. When radio personality Paul Harvey did a segment about the product on his national news show, Zoo

Doo's toll-free telephone number began ringing and didn't stop. "People wanted to buy it for themselves, for their friends, or maybe as a joke for some in-laws they didn't like," Ledbetter says. "I was on the phone all day the first day, and the phone company later said that more than 16,000 people tried to get through."

Ledbetter's initial idea evolved around people coming to the zoo and buying baskets of the compost. Because thousands of baskets are used to contain and carry the animals' food, this presented another way to recycle. But when the idea took off, he soon began selling Zoo Doo through the mail in 1-, 5-, and 15-pound buckets.

Pierce Ledbetter succeeded at turning the expensive job of disposing zoo animals' waste into a profitable and eco-friendly project.

An elephant at the Memphis Zoo holds a bucket of Zoo Doo.

A dozen American zoos now participate in the Zoo Doo effort, including the famous San Diego (California) Zoo. The zoos end up saving thousands of dollars each year by not having to haul tons of the manure to a landfill every day, and they also receive a large percentage of the profits made from selling the Zoo Doo.

"The zoos didn't realize how much they were spending on disposing of these wastes," Ledbetter explains. "An average zoo sells $12,000 worth of Zoo Doo a year with little effort, but ends up saving thousands more in landfill fees." In addition, gardeners benefit from the high quality of this compost product. Zoo Doo is produced from a highly controlled waste stream; no sick or meat-eating animals are used.

"But awareness of composting is the best thing we've accomplished," Ledbetter adds. "Zoo waste is tiny compared to the amount of yard wastes that go to landfills every year. The zoos set up composting exhibits to show kids how easy it is to compost at home. And there's no better tool than an elephant's rear end to create awareness and humor about composting. It's so much more exciting than a rotting pile of leaves."

For More Information

Write to Zoo Doo Compost Company, 281 East Parkway, North Greenhouse Division, Memphis, TN 38112, or call (800) I LUV DOO (458–8366).

The Invisible Gardener

Andy Lopez goes to work with a bottle of Tabasco sauce, vinegar, a bag of flour, garlic cloves—and peppermint soap. He may sound like a strange Cajun chef, but he's actually one of the most respected organic gardeners in the world. He uses these items as pesticides.

As time passes, more and more supposedly "safe" chemicals are being outlawed. In each case, society unknowingly has served as the guinea pig. That's why Andy Lopez promotes organic alternatives through books, radio shows, tapes, and lectures. "Peppermint soap, for instance, is toxic to insects and ants," he explains. "It scrambles their senses and drives them away. I put Dr. Bronner's Peppermint Soap in water and spray it on plants and vegetables. It's also good for many plant diseases, but it has to be the right concentration—about one tablespoon per gallon."

Vinegar also works well in gardens. Many plants thrive on it as a nutritional supplement and quickly absorb it. And when poured in a bowl, it can attract and kill pests. "Just cover a bowl of vinegar with some lettuce leaves and place it in your garden. Vinegar attracts snails and other creatures that are predators by nature. It's a good trap. If you're getting lots of the same type of pest, you probably have an infestation problem. If you're capturing a wide variety of pests, however, then your garden population is probably balanced, and that's usually a good sign. In this case, remove the bowl of vinegar. The key is balance. All creatures have a place," he comments.

Wheat flour is another organic alternative for gardeners. When poured around the base of plants, it creates a temporary

A young gardener shows off a huge head of lettuce grown with the Invisible Gardener technique.

barrier against most crawling creatures—especially when mixed with cayenne pepper. When mixed with compost, wheat flour forms an excellent patch for cut and scarred trees. Liquid mixtures of water, garlic, and cayenne pepper also are extremely effective against various pests when sprayed directly on the plant. "It's really very simple. The philosophy is to help Mother Nature heal herself," Lopez says.

Lopez has been interested in organic growing methods all his life. Growing up in Puerto Rico and Cuba, his mother always had a compost pile and used other resourceful practices. He never knew any different. When he was looking for a way to finance his education at the University of Colorado in Boulder, he started a night-time gardening business. Organic, of course. "That's how I got the nickname 'Invisible Gardener'— my clients would wake up in the morning and see an entirely different garden without ever seeing me."

Lopez stresses that the key to organic pest control, and to gardening in general, is healthy soil. To protect the soil, he warns people not to go overboard when controlling pests organically. "You don't want to sterilize the place," he warns. Gardeners must also carefully read the labels of the products they use, since many products claim to be organic or natural when they really aren't.

Lopez currently runs a business and an association of organic gardeners under the Invisible Gardener name, but he stresses that "Invisible" now refers to the environmental impact of the organic practice. He has written two books on the subject: *How to Heal the Earth In Your Spare Time* and *Natural Pest Control, Alternatives to Chemical Pest Control for the Home and Garden, Farmer and Professional*.

In addition, Lopez has a radio talk show and publishes four newsletters a year. What is more, he manages a help line and an on-line bulletin-board service. On top of all this, the Invisible Gardener even makes house calls around the world, providing his gardening expertise to both homeowners and professionals.

Today, Lopez's Invisible Gardeners of America is an international association that boasts more than 6,000 members. The club provides information to its members on the various methods of organic pest control and natural pet care. "The club provides information that promotes a healthier, cleaner lifestyle," Lopez says. "We act as a sort of 'Seal of Organic Approval.' If it's not organic, we know it and we will tell you." The Invisible Gardeners of America offers organic products, tapes, classes, workshops, and training. Its members also work with children of all ages to help them understand how to care for the Earth.

For More Information

Write to the Invisible Gardener, P.O. Box 4311, Malibu, CA 90264, or call (800) 354–9296.

"Green" Products and Packaging

*A*griculture that has a positive effect on the environment and organic gardening are two areas of importance that we have looked at. Corporations can also make a tremendous impact on the environment—for the better, or for the worse. When it comes to environmental efforts, all corporations are *not* created equal. Some go out of their way to help minimize the pollution they produce, while others avoid complying with local and national environmental regulations. Some companies exploit the environment for every extra penny of profit, while others spend generously to protect the environment or even share their profits with conservation organizations. The stories in this chapter are proof that profit making and environmentalism can go hand-in-hand. In fact, environmentalism can even be a competitive advantage to a company.

A Natural Approach to Business

From its beginnings, Tom's of Maine has made environmentalism one of its cornerstones. In 1968, the company's founders, Tom and Kate Chappell moved from Philadelphia, Pennsylvania, to rural Maine, as part of their plan to get back in touch with nature. They ate natural foods and used natural products whenever possible. But they were unable to find any natural personal-care products. This gave them an idea for a new company.

The Chappells' first product, called Clearlake, was the nation's first nonphosphate liquid laundry detergent. At the time, wastewater containing phosphate (abrasive chemicals) was causing algae to choke many rivers in America. The Chappells started by peddling their product in the early morning hours to dairy farmers and other area residents. They encouraged customers to recycle their empty Clearlake containers by mailing them back—postage paid—to be refilled by the couple.

The Chappells soon created a whole line of personal-care products, and Tom's of Maine was born. In 1975, Tom's Natural Spearmint Toothpaste was made. The company now also produces deodorant, shampoo, soap, mouthwash, shaving cream, and dental floss. Natural ingredients play an extremely important role at Tom's of Maine. For instance, the artificial sweetener saccharin is found in all major brands of toothpaste except Tom's, where cinnamon, spearmint, and peppermint oils are used instead.

41

With co-worker Danielle Smith-Bouthot, Tom Chappell discusses the company's educational information on its packaging.

From its modest door-to-door beginnings, Tom's of Maine has grown to become a $20 million-per-year company. It is still privately owned and its products are now sold all around the world.

"We care about the environment and we live that commitment. We have strong respect for nature and people. It starts with our corporate mission, which drives the company's philosophy and strategies," Chappell says. "It's about trying to do the right thing—being financially responsible while being environmentally sensitive and socially responsible."

Concern for the environment is evident in all Tom's of Maine products. For example, the company's toothpaste tubes are recyclable, because they are made of aluminum. All other Tom's packaging is made from 100 percent recycled materials. In addition, the company is now offering the first refillable roll-on deodorant packaging, resulting in a 20-percent reduction in solid waste. "We eliminated the outer packaging from our mouthwash products and just attached an accordion booklet to the container to convey our messages. This reduced packaging by 90 percent, which reduced our costs. In turn, we were able to lower the cost to our customers," Chappell says.

Tom's of Maine contributes 10 percent of its profits to nonprofit organizations. Three such projects in Brazil are designed to encourage preservation of the rainforest through research and development of medicinal rainforest plants. By developing sustainable harvesting practices, economic alternatives can be created for people while saving the rainforest.

In addition, Tom's of Maine products do not contain animal ingredients and are tested for safety without the use of animals. Tom's requires a written guarantee from all of its suppliers that none of the ingredients supplied to the company are tested on animals.

Chappell's efforts have gained attention and respect. In June 1995, he won the Socially Responsible New England Entrepreneur of the Year Award, sponsored by *Inc.* magazine. "Other nominees came from companies that were bigger and growing faster," he explains. It shows that the way you do business is important."

Chappell is confident that his ethical approach to business is rubbing off on other companies. He believes that most companies do care about the environment, communities, and society. When they can see a prosperous, non-traditional company responding to society's values, it encourages them to move in that direction. "If a company truly cares about the environment, it has to go the extra mile," Chappell notes. "As Tom's of Maine gets bigger, we'll make a bigger impact on society."

For More Information

Write to Tom's of Maine, P.O. Box 710, Kennebunk, ME 04043, or call (800) 367–8667.

Juice Maker Reduces Impact on the Environment

Environmentalism is a profitable management tool for one of America's oldest juice makers. Veryfine Products of Westford, Massachusetts, has sold bottled fruit juice since 1865. Protecting natural resources is an important part of Veryfine's operations. These efforts save the company about $600,000 a year.

In 1995, for instance, the company recycled 95 percent of its solid waste, which saved it substantial landfill and transportation costs. "My goal is to eventually have zero solid-waste discharge," Bill Lindsey, director of Environmental Affairs, says. "As tall of an order as that is, I feel it's achievable."

To this end, the company introduced the first drink container in America to use post-consumer recycled plastic. It also uses as much recycled glass and aluminum as possible for its "green" containers—about 45 to 50 percent recycled content. "We'd prefer to use 100 percent recycled aluminum and glass because it costs less to process," Lindsey says. "But there's just not enough recycled aluminum and glass available, and there won't be until we have more mandatory curbside recycling programs."

On another environmental front, Veryfine reduces its energy consumption by recycling heat generated during its bottle-production process in order to warm its 500,000-square-foot warehouse. The company also disposes of more than 3,000 tons of apple waste annually, giving it to local farmers, who use it as animal feed. The farmers only have to pay transportation costs.

Veryfine's efforts have impressed more than just its accountants and stockholders. The company has also won ten environmental awards for its efforts. "The award I'm most proud of came from the Massachusetts Audubon Society," says Lindsey. "It was one of the first awards that they had ever given to a corporation."

Veryfine began its environmental program in the 1970s, and it continues to expand the program every year. Its experience shows that companies should not be afraid of being environmentally proactive. Environmentalism can help them save money, and it can help them make money.

"We've been described as a model for other corporations, so we actively promote environmentalism to other businesses through speaking and consulting," Lindsey says. "Companies that aren't concerned about their environmental impact probably won't be around in the twenty-first century."

The Massachusetts Audubon Society gave its highest award to Veryfine for its leadership in the business community on environmental issues.

For More Information

Write to Veryfine Products, Inc., P.O. Box 670, Westford, MA 01886, or call (800) VERYFINE.

Sat Sontokh Khalsa was concerned about the destruction of the world's rainforests. In thinking about the best way to get information on the subject to as many people as possible, he thought of printing it on the back of cereal boxes—because *everybody* reads those. And so a cereal company was formed in 1989, when Khalsa, assisted by Steve Bogoff, began Rainforest Products in Mill Valley, California.

The company now makes five different cereals—Rainforest Granola, Rainforest Crisp, Rainforest Flakes & Honey Nut Clusters, Cinnamon Rainforest Puffs, and Honey Rainforest Puffs. Rainforest Products supports rainforest residents in their efforts to earn their livelihood through the sale of nuts and fruits and other products. In this way, they can afford to continue their traditional lifestyle and prevent logging and ranching from taking over their land. Production of sustainably harvested, shelled Brazil nuts (as opposed to destroying the source of the product) has gone from 32,000 pounds in 1990 to 386,000 pounds in 1993. Rainforest Products accounts for about one fourth of the total. This model has moved throughout the Amazon Basin as well as into Guinea Bissau, Cambodia, and Vietnam. In addition to Brazil nuts, Rainforest Products currently buys sustainably harvested cinnamon from Sumatra in Indonesia and sustainably harvested honey from the Maya in the Yucatan Peninsula in Mexico.

"It has become pretty clear that for the rainforest to remain intact, there needs to be people who have a vested interest in

being there and who can defend their land," Khalsa says. "In order for people to be able to live there, they have to be able to afford to live there. To me, 'sustainable' means something different from what it means to a lot of people. It means that it has to be sustainable not only ecologically, but economically as well. People in the rainforest have to make enough money to be able to stay where they are and protect their land and the ecosystem."

Cinnamon, which has just been harvested and bundled, is carried out of the forest of Sumatra.

The company's cereals can now be found on the shelves of thousands of grocery stores around the country. Many are health-food stores, but a smattering of mainstream grocery stores have begun to carry the products. Last year, Rainforest Crisp was the fifth-best-selling cereal in southern California health-food stores, and sales continue to grow.

"We are in the unique position of having a product for sale about which we can truly say that the more we sell, the more we serve the rainforests and the people who dwell in them," Khalsa says. "We hope to use our involvement in the marketplace to help people understand the vital impact that stopping rainforest destruction has on the survival of humankind."

For More Information
Write to RF Cereals, P.O. Box 9998, Berkeley, CA 94709, or call (510) 548–3325.

Nature's Products

Mother Nature has always provided humans with the basic substances necessary to sustain life. Our ancestors learned that certain plants had medicinal values, while others were valued for their nutritional elements. They also learned that some plants had pleasant aromas, while others were poisonous. With the Industrial Revolution, however, came the quest to improve on many of the things that nature already supplied. Chemicals and machinery soon replaced many natural ingredients and human workers. Pollution and natural resource depletion quickly became issues that people had to consider. Today, many people have returned to the basics—using the products that come directly from Mother Nature, which don't require much processing or packaging. These natural products can minimize pollution and help conserve our natural resources.

Uncle Sam's Medicine Man

Dr. James Duke, senior economic botanist for the U.S. Department of Agriculture, has studied medicinal plants, including herbs, for more than 30 years. When he looks at the world's rainforests, he sees the potential for new medicines, new jobs, and a reason to preserve the forests. "I have a great interest in helping tropical countries develop their medicinal plants while conserving their forests," says Duke. "Two decades ago, most chemists anticipated that the majority of modern medicines could be produced synthetically [artificially]. But that hasn't happened. About 25 percent of our modern medicines are still derived from, or patterned after, plant chemicals. In fact, aspirin, the most commonly used medicine in the world, originally came from a plant." In the United States, it now costs about $360 million to get a new drug screened, tested for safety, and approved for effectiveness. It generally takes about ten years to get a new drug on the market.

Only 2 percent of the world's rainforests have been thoroughly researched for potential medicinal plants. Many treasures may still be hidden there. Countless species of plants may have already been lost forever in areas of destroyed forest. Every nation in the world could benefit from new medicinal discoveries, and developing countries could benefit economically. "I now have a list of 100 existing medicinal compounds found in the rainforests of the world," Duke says. "Most of these compounds are currently produced in the First World [developed countries], but most could be produced and refined in the tropics. In many cases, this would lower the cost of production and improve developing economies, which would take some of the local pressures away from rainforest destruction." But an inventory of plant species in the rainforests needs to be completed. Duke plans to start screening many of the most promising plant species to determine their effects on various diseases.

The botanist says that he relies heavily on his instincts to spot plants with medicinal potential. "You can tell when a plant has a distinct odor or when its stinging nettle causes an immediate reaction," he says. "But one of the best screens is what the local people know. I like to study the plants that they say are either medicinal or poison. Very often, the poisonous ones can be medicinal when applied appropriately."

In the world of ethnobotany (the study of plants and how they are used around the world), Duke is known as "Uncle Sam's Medicine Man." He has done research in many parts of the world, including China. But most of his work has been done in Latin America. Duke reports, "I collected about 10,000 specimens in Panama, and about 40 of those species were previously unknown to science."

In 1993, after an introductory trip to the rainforests of Sumatra, Indonesia, Duke's imagination ran wild. He saw plants that were new to him and possibly the entire medicinal world. "As I familiarized myself with the plant life in Sumatra, I couldn't help but wonder how many unknown species were within my reach. These unknown plants could possibly cure cancer or other mysterious diseases," he exclaims. Duke wants to start working closely with the Indonesian government to take a thorough inventory of the country's forests.

The search for medicinal plants is also under way in North America's wild lands and forests. These areas hold medicinal treasures that must be protected and researched. Unfortunately, many herbs found in North America are being harvested too quickly in order to serve the growing market for alternative medicines. This careless harvesting method destroys the natural crops, making regeneration difficult. To help promote the research, use, and conservation of some of these herbal species, Duke serves on the advisory board of the Herbal Research

Foundation—an internationally recognized center for herbal research and education.

Dr. Duke (left) inspects plant life on Sumatra with the help of local Indonesians.

Herbs are often effective at weakening a virus or disease while strengthening the patient. The mayapple, for instance, contains a promising treatment for one type of lung cancer. In 1992, the market for this medicinal compound exceeded $275 million. "Lots of people are using the cone flower, too, because it's known for boosting the immune system," Duke says. Another herb, bloodroot, is effective against plaque on teeth. As a result of its newly found popularity, this herb is already threatened in parts of North Carolina.

"Some people see medicinal plants becoming the Microsoft industry of the next decade," he says. "I hope they're right—but even more plant species will become endangered if the growth isn't properly managed."

For More Information

Write to the Herbal Research Foundation, 1007 Pearl Street, Suite 200, Boulder, CO 80302, or call (303) 449–2265.

Traditional Healers Provide Clues to New Drugs

The search for new medicines may be an effective way to help conserve the remaining forests of the world. About 25 percent of modern medicines are derived from plants, many of which were discovered by working with traditional healers. Just a fraction of the world's plants have been tested for medicinal potential. Childhood leukemia, for instance, can be treated with a drug derived from the Madagascar periwinkle flower.

Given this potential to save lives and ecosystems with medicinal plants, Shaman Pharmaceuticals is going to its namesake—shamans, or traditional healers—to discover rain-forest plants that it can use to develop new drugs. Shaman's mission is to develop a more efficient drug-discovery process by isolating compounds from tropical plants with a history of medicinal use by the indigenous people of a region. The company also strives to help the people it contacts during these searches by promoting development of the rainforests in ways that don't destroy them.

"We're looking for medicines used by traditional healers, and in doing so we're working directly with indigenous people from all over the world," says Steven King, Shaman's vice-president of Ethnobotany and Conservation. "Because these local people have been using these medicinal plants for years— and sometimes centuries—we can be fairly certain that they are effective and don't have extreme side effects."

Using a team of ethnobotanists, the company visits indigenous groups in many of the world's rainforests. Through this

Steven King (left) and Thomas Carlson (right) learn from Elias Gualinga, a Quechua healer in Ecuador.

process, the company has "discovered" two drugs that are now in the process of being approved by the U.S. Food and Drug Administration. Provir is used to combat traveler's diarrhea and possibly cholera. The drug's active ingredient was isolated in a medicinal plant that grows abundantly in South America. Human clinical trials are now under way for the substance. The second one, called Virend, is a skin formula used to treat herpes. Shaman Pharmaceuticals discovered the plant used to make this drug by showing pictures of herpes infections to healers in Ecuador and the Amazon River Basin. The healers simply brought out a certain plant and said this is what they

53

used to treat that ailment. Other pharmaceutical drugs currently in use that have tropical-plant origins include pilocarpine, used to treat glaucoma; quinine, used to fight malaria; and vinblastine, used to treat certain cancers.

When Shaman Pharmaceuticals approaches a group of people to start a medicinal search, the company finds out what it can provide the community to help them in return for their efforts. Requests have included a new water system, a longer airstrip, and regular visits from dentists and physicians.

Once a plant material is found and screened, it is exported to America from Latin America, Southeast Asia, or Africa. Shaman requires that all plant collections be done in a sustainable manner, which can include replanting in areas of intensive harvesting. The company policy also requires that each plant targeted for large-scale production must have multicountry sources of supply or have the ability to be made synthetically. This policy reduces the risks that are sometimes associated with using foreign suppliers, such as political or climate instability. A diverse supply also minimizes the chance of species extinction from overharvesting.

Shaman Pharmaceutical's drug-discovery team focuses on local people's recognition of common symptoms. Team members avoid using terms such as "malaria" and "parasites," which might be recognized by locals and influence their responses. The goal of Shaman's method is to identify plants used to treat certain symptoms and collect them for analysis. Additional collections and observations are made when the local shaman provides health care to local people. "When useful plants are discovered and products made, we will provide a portion of the profits from any and all of our products to the cultures and countries in which we have worked," King comments.

In the long term, the company helps communities by providing them with a way to harvest products from the rainforest without destroying it. "One of the threats to the environment is poverty—people are responsible for either managing or destroying the rainforests," King explains. "We're giving governments a reason to protect their resources and local people a way to make a profit off non-timber products. We need to give local people alternatives to selling their forests."

In 1990, Shaman created the Healing Forest Conservancy to provide more help to indigenous people. This nonprofit coservation organization—funded in part with Shaman Pharmaceutical profits—provides money for schools and medical services in different parts of the world, including areas where the company is not working. The foundation believes that educating people in areas that they don't have experience in can also help preserve biodiversity over time.

For More Information

Write to Shaman Pharmaceuticals or Healing Forest Conservancy, 213 East Grand Avenue, South San Francisco, CA 94080–4812, or call (415) 952–7070.

Rainforest Buttons

The Tagua Initiative® (TI), is a joint project between Conservation International (CI) and its local Ecuadorian counterpart CIDESA. The effort uses tagua nuts sustainably harvested from the rainforest of northwestern Ecuador to make buttons, carvings, and jewelry. The distributors licensed by TI have sold more than 35 million buttons in the United States, Asia, and Europe to clothing manufacturers such as The Gap and Smith & Hawken.

Money from these sales helps to fund all aspects of the project. In turn, the effort helps people in parts of rural Ecuador and Colombia earn a living and protect the rainforest.

The first area where TI began operating was in the Comuna Río Santiago-Cayapas (CRS), an Afro-Ecuadoran community of 15,000 people. The CRS is one of the poorest areas of Ecuador. Incomes are well below the national average, and services such as health care, water, and education are inadequate or even nonexistent. Economic activity revolves around cutting timber, cattle ranching, and harmful agriculural practices.

The Tagua Initiative® offers local people an alternative to these destructive activities. Community members involved with TI harvest

Some of the end results of CI's conservation efforts are these beautiful hand-made tagua buttons.

tagua nuts from the floor of the rainforest and sell them to 1 of 12 TI buying centers. These buying centers are managed by groups of people from the communities that have been trained in business administration and marketing. The buying centers process the tagua and sell it to factories in Manta, Ecuador. Today, TI sells more than 20 different tagua products in 8 countries worldwide. Conservation International is exploring other new, diverse markets for tagua nuts, such as charcoal, abrasives, and other gift items, such as wine corks, clocks, and drawer pulls.

Employing more than 1,800 people in Ecuador alone, TI provides income to over 625 families in the region through the harvest and sale of the tagua. The extra money and the environmental education programs that the project has brought into the community have helped to slow the destruction of the rainforest. "Deforestation of the rainforests is driven in part by lack of alternatives for local people. We want to offer viable economic solutions that will help these communities in the long run and save the rainforest ecosystem," explains Robin Frank, a director of CI's Enterprise Department and the Tagua Initiative.

Scientific research and sound economic principles underlie all of CI's conservation efforts. The organization's mission is to help both the environment and local people by linking conservation efforts with economic needs. "The Tagua Initiative is a perfect example of how this type of conservation effort works," notes Frank. "If we can manage the rainforest and provide income and jobs for the local people year after year, these projects will make a difference."

The organization is now developing other sustainable rainforest products throughout Latin America, Asia, and Africa. For example, CI is working in Guatemala with Croda, Inc., a worldwide leader in developing cosmetics, to market three forest products in the United States to be used in personal-care items, such as shampoo, soap, and lotion. The project employs people living in and around the Maya Biosphere Reserve, the

A worker peels tagua nuts in Ecuador as part of the initial processing of the nuts.

largest tract of rainforest left in Central America. The products—cohune oil, allspice oil, and jabancillo extract—are helping local Guatemalan communities earn money in a sustainable, non-destructive way.

Local people harvest cohune nuts from palm trees in the Petén region of Guatemala. Community members then press the nuts in a machine to remove the oil, which can be used as a substitute for coconut or African palm oil—two ingredients commonly found in personal-care products. Allspice oil comes from the allspice tree. After harvesting the leaves of the tree, local people dry the leaves, and Croda workers rinse them to remove the fragrant oil that cosmetics companies often use in lip balms and skin creams. The community obtains jabancillo extract from the dried red berries of the jabancillo plant. This rose-colored liquid extract foams in water and was used by the ancient Maya to make soap. Today, the personal-care industry uses jabancillo extract for facial washes and other kinds of soap.

"Collecting nuts and berries won't save the rainforest in and of itself, but the efforts are tools for conservation," comments Sharon Flynn, a director of Conservation Enterprises at CI. "By creating jobs and demonstrating how the rainforest can be used sustainably and left intact, we are supporting other strategies that can make a difference, such as education, land-rights issues, and other community-based efforts."

For More Information
Write to Conservation International, 1015 18th Street NW, Suite 1000, Washington, D.C. 20036, or call (202) 429–5660.

Natural Deodorant from Asia

For centuries, people in Thailand have used natural mineral salts to purify their water and keep their bodies clean. The salts kill the various forms of bacteria that hamper water quality and cause body odors. Now those salts are available in the United States in the form of the Thai Deodorant Stone. One stone is equal to more than a dozen cans of deodorant spray and is 100 percent natural—containing no harsh chemicals, perfumes, oils, or emulsifiers (substances that make other deodorants stick to the skin).

"The stones dissolve completely, so there's no plastic, no container, no waste," says Marsha Joseph of Deodorant Stones of America, a Phoenix, Arizona-based company. "And there's no spray to harm the ozone layer."

Users simply moisten the stone and glide it on like any roll-on deodorant. The stones are not sticky or greasy and will not stain clothing, and they are safe for the body because the salts are not absorbed into the skin. In addition to using them on your underarms, the stones can be used everywhere on the body, such as on the feet, or even for acne.

To create the product in Thailand, selected soils are sifted to attain high concentrations of potassium and other mineral salts. The salts are then crystallized in a liquid solution and eventually are dried and formed into large blocks. Individual stones are then hand-cut, smoothed, and shaped from the larger blocks. Mineral-salt crystals left over from the production of the deodorant stones are recycled and used in Thailand to

Larry Morris oversees a batch of deodorant stones being smoothed and shaped in the factory in Thailand.

purify water. Currently, the deodorant stones are sold in various health-food stores and in some other stores. To date, more than 3 million of the stones have been sold in the United States.

Deodorant Stones of America was started by Larry Morris in 1986, after a man he had just met—who was then living in Thailand—told him about the product. They soon joined together to start the company. After Morris borrowed $15,000 from a family member, his new partner went back to Thailand to set up their factory. During the first year, fewer than 1,000 stones were sold, but the partners kept working, and sales slowly grew. Now, more than 1 million stones are sold internationally every year.

For More Information

Write to Deodorant Stones of America, 9420 East Doubletree Ranch Road, Suite 101, Scottsdale, AZ 85258, or call (800) 279-9318.

These are just a few of the great success stories about natural foods and products. With a little research, you can find other exciting examples around the world and possibly even in your own hometown. We hope that this book inspires you to continue learning as much as possible.

Glossary

biodiversity The combined diversity of plant and animal species on Earth.

biointensive The practice of maximizing the natural impact of a product or process.

botanist A scientist who studies plants.

compost A mixture that consists largely of decayed organic matter and is used for conditioning and fertilizing land; composting is the process of making this mixture.

developing world Nations in the process, to varying degrees, of industrializing their economics.

ecosystem A community and its environment functioning as a unit in nature.

entomology The study of insects.

ethics A set of moral principles and disciplines.

ethnobotany The study of cultures and their use of plants around the world.

food chain The order in which organisms feed on one another in an ecosystem.

herbs A plant or plant part valued for its medicinal or aromatic qualities.

indigenous A species or subspecies, including humans, originating from a particular region.

insecticide A toxic substance used to kill insects.

manure Solid animal excrement (waste).

ozone layer An atmospheric layer about 20 to 30 miles above the Earth consisting of high levels of ozone. It serves as a screen to keep harmful levels of radiation from reaching the Earth.

parasite An organism living in or on another organism.

pollination When pollen is transferred from a plant's stamen to an ovule.

shaman A traditional healer who relies on the use of plants, herbs, and rituals to cure the sick.

sludge A muddy or slushy mass of sediment; solid matter from water or sewage treatment.

sustainable harvesting Harvesting a food or product without damaging or destroying the ecosystem.

synthetic Something that is produced artificially.

UNICEF The United Nations Children's Emergency Fund; now commonly known as the United Nations Children's Fund.

Further Reading

Banks, Martin. *Conserving Rain Forests.* Chatham, NJ: Raintree Steck-Vaughn, 1990.

Glaser, Linda. *Compost: From Garbage to Gardens.* Brookfield, CT: Millbrook Press, 1996.

Huff, Barbara. *Greening the City Streets: The Story of Community Gardens.* Boston, MA: Clarion Books, 1990.

Kerrod, Robin. *The Environment.* Tarrytown, NY: Marshall Cavendish, 1993.

Lambert, Mark. *Farming and the Environment.* Chatham, NJ: Raintree Steck-Vaughn, 1990.

Landau, Elaine. *Environmental Groups: The Earth Savers.* Springfield, NJ: Enslow Publishers, 1993.

Pringle, Laurence. *Living Treasure: Saving Earth's Threatened Biodiversity.* New York: Morrow Junior Books, 1991.

Willis, Terri. *Land Use and Abuse.* Danbury, CT: Children's Press, 1992.

Index

Photo Credits

Cover and pages 8, 9: Cary S. Wolinsky; page 12: ©CNRI/Science Photo Library/Photo Researchers, Inc.; page 14: Wheelabrator Water Technologies—Bio Gro Division; page 16: ©Sean Sprague; pages 17, 18: courtesy of Thanksgiving Coffee Company; page 20: courtesy of Coffee Kids; page 23: ©1993 George Rose/Fetzer Vineyards; page 26: Robert Gerheart/Rodale Press, Inc.; page 29: ©1994 Cynthia Raiser Jeavons; page 30: ©1995 Cynthia Raiser Jeavons; page 32: ©Frank J. Sudol; pages 35, 36: Zoo Doo Compost Company; page 38: Invisible Gardener; page 42: Tom's of Maine; page 45: ©David Zadig/Massachusetts Audobon Society; page 47: ©Thomas Fricke; page 51: Gary Chandler/EarthNEWS; pages 53, 54: Steven King; pages 56, 58: ©Haroldo Castro/Conservation International; page 60: Deodarant Stones of America.